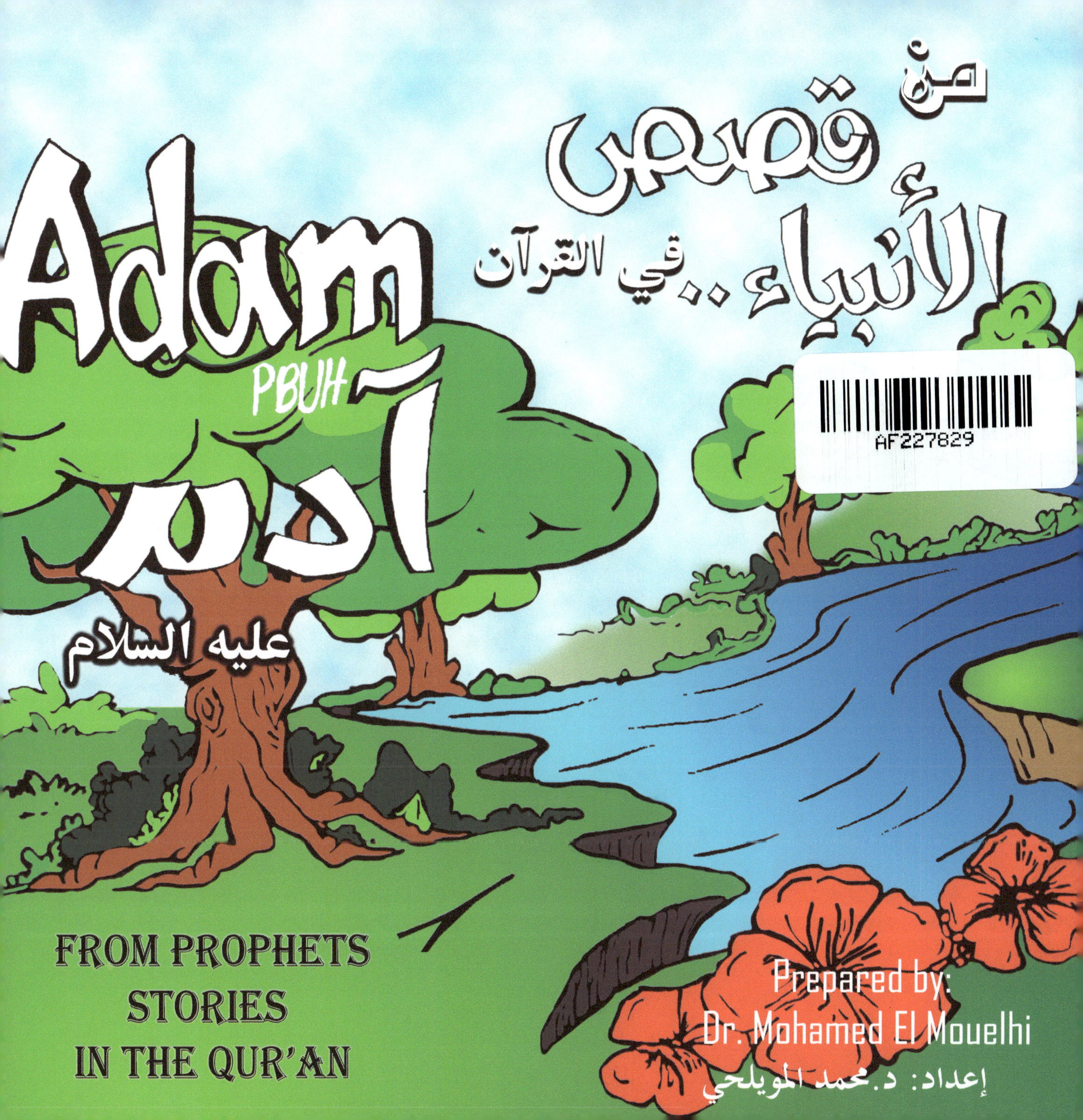

مِن قصصى الأنبياء.. في القرآن
Adam
PBUH
آدم
عليه السلام
FROM PROPHETS
STORIES
IN THE QUR'AN
AF227829
Prepared by:
Dr. Mohamed El Mouelhi
إعداد: د. محمد المويلحي

ISBN 978-1-7357701-5-4

First edition 2021

Published by Honey Elm Books LLC
www.HoneyElmBooks.com

Adam PBUH

آدم عليه السلام

Editing: Noha Elmouelhi

Artistic Preparation:

Hossam El Mouelhi - Donia Farouk - Joud El Mouelhi

تحرير: نهى المويلحي

الإعداد الفني: حسام المويلحي – دنيا فاروق – جود المويلحي

The history of humanity started with the creation
of Adam by Almighty God.
Allah gave Adam special status over the Angels by giving him
the ability to think, to learn, to tell the difference between
right and wrong, and freedom of choice.
Allah gave Adam special knowledge
and taught him about His creations.

بدأت قصة البشرية بأن خلق الله آدم عليه السلام من طين،
وقد أصطفاه على جميع مخلوقاته بما فيهم الملائكة بقدرته على
التعلم والعقل والمقدرة على التمييز بين الصواب والخطأ
وكذلك القدرة على الإختيار. وبعد أن خلق الله آدم لقنه
العلم المفيد له والذى ميز آدم به دون الملائكة.

One day, Allah ordered the Angels to bow to Adam
as an indication of his higher status.
This was a great honor for mankind,
and we should remind ourselves to do good deeds
in order to be deserving of it.

وزيادة فى تكريم الإنسان
أمر الله الملائكة بالسجود لآدم تعظيماً لمكانته الخاصة
وتميزه حتى عن الملائكة، ويا له من تكريم عظيم للإنسان،
يجب علينا جميعاً أن نذكِّر أنفسنا بها وأن نكون أهلا لها.

All of the Angels followed Allah's order
and bowed to Adam, but Iblis refused and disobeyed
Allah's command.
Iblis was very arrogant and felt that he was better than Adam
who had been created from clay while he had been created from fire.
Iblis grew jealous of Allah's preference for Adam.

وأستجاب كل الملائكة لأمر الله بالسجود لآدم، ولكن إبليس
رفض السجود لآدم وعصى أمرالله.
وكانت حجة إبليس أنه أفضل من آدم المخلوق من طين
بينما هو مخلوق من نار.
وتكبر إبليس لغيرته من تفضيل الله لآدم وتكريمه عليه.

"Allah said: `What prevented you to prostrate to Adam,
when I commanded you?'
Iblis said: `I am better than him, You created me from fire,
and You created him from clay.' "

(Al-Araf: 12)

بِسْمِ اللّهِ الرَّحْمَنِ الرَّحِيمِ

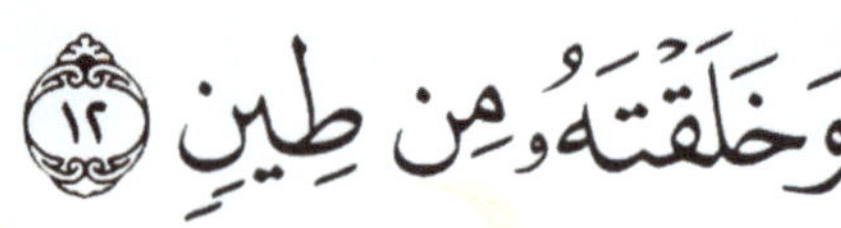

قَالَ مَا مَنَعَكَ أَلَّا تَسْجُدَ إِذْ أَمَرْتُكَ قَالَ أَنَا خَيْرٌ مِّنْهُ خَلَقْتَنِي مِن نَّارٍ وَخَلَقْتَهُ مِن طِينٍ ﴿١٢﴾

Adam lived in Paradise (Heaven) but he felt lonely.

Allah created Hawa to be his companion and wife.

Adam and Hawa lived together in Paradise

and enjoyed their time there.

However, Allah told them that they could enjoy everything in Paradise

but He warned them to not eat from a specific tree. Allah wanted to test

them and see if they would obey Him.

وكان آدم يشعر بالوحدة وهو في الجنة فخلق الله له زوجته حواء حتى يستأنس بها

ويتمتعا معا بالعيش في الجنة، وأسكنهما الله الجنة.

وأمرهما الله أن يتمتعا بكل نعم الجنة

ولكن لا يأكلا من شجرة معينة كأختبار لهما لطاعة أوامر الله.

It seemed an easy enough order to follow.
As time passed, Adam forgot what had happened
with Iblis and his disobedience to Allah.
But of course, Iblis was still jealous of Adam and wanted to get even.

وقد يبدو أمراً بسيطاً وسهلاً، ولكن آدم نسى موقف إبليس وعداوته له،
ولكن إبليس لم ينسى تفضيل الله لآدم عليه،
وصمم على دفع آدم الى معصية الله سبحانه وتعالى حتى يتساوا فى المعصية.

"And We said: `O Adam! Dwell you and your wife
in the Paradise and eat both of you freely
with pleasure and delight,
of things therein as wherever you will,
but come not near this tree or you both will be of the wrong-doers.' "

(Al-Baqara: 35)

سُورَةُ الْبَقَرَةِ

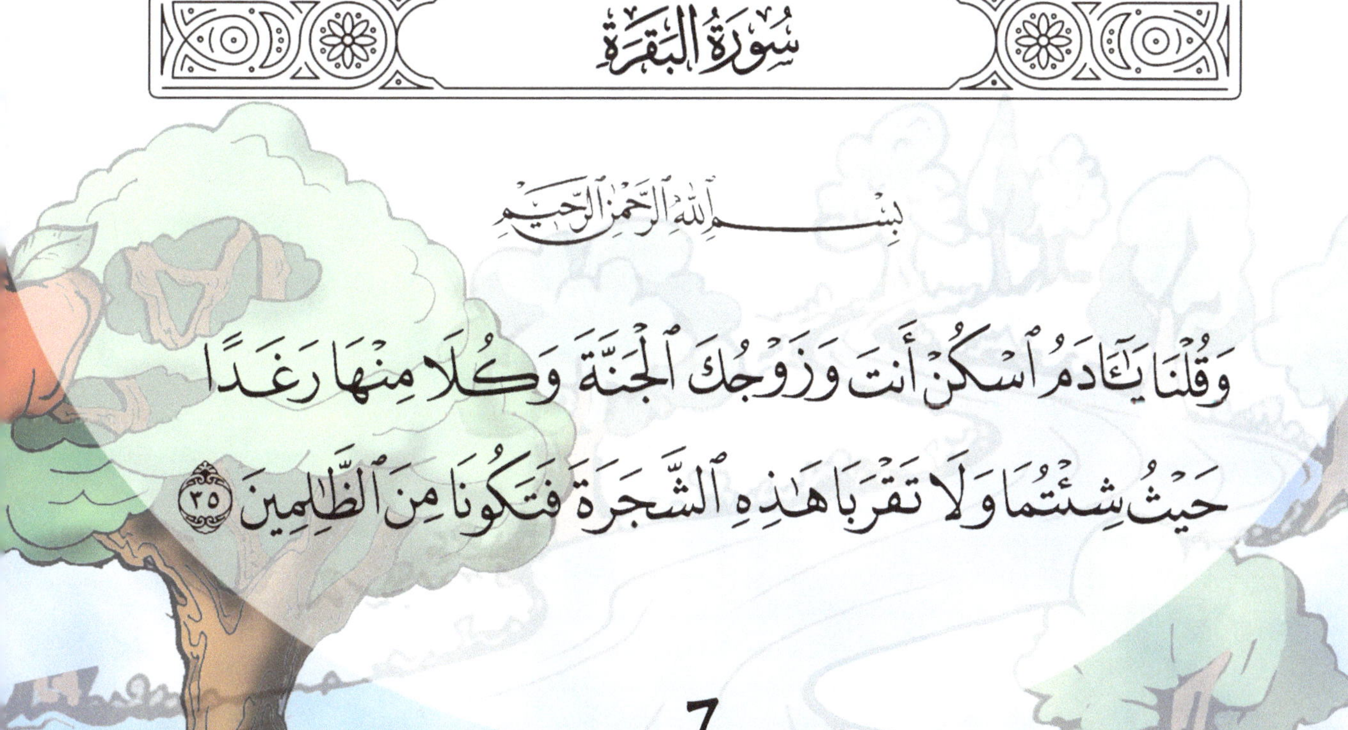

بِسْمِ اللَّهِ الرَّحْمَٰنِ الرَّحِيمِ

وَقُلْنَا يَٰٓـَٔادَمُ ٱسْكُنْ أَنتَ وَزَوْجُكَ ٱلْجَنَّةَ وَكُلَا مِنْهَا رَغَدًا حَيْثُ شِئْتُمَا وَلَا تَقْرَبَا هَٰذِهِ ٱلشَّجَرَةَ فَتَكُونَا مِنَ ٱلظَّٰلِمِينَ ۞

Iblis kept thinking of how he could make Adam disobey Allah.

Iblis decided to trick Adam and Hawa by persuading them how great it would be if they ate the fruit of the forbidden tree.

They didn't listen to him.

Iblis didn't give up and kept trying to convince them.

وأخذ إبليس يفكر كيف يدفع آدم الى المعصية، فقرر أن يقنعهما بأن ثمار الشجرة التى حرم الله أن يأكلا منها إنما هى شجرة الخلد، ولكن آدم وحواء لم يستمعا له، ولم ييأس إبليس وأستمر فى محاولاته.

Iblis swore to them that this tree was a special tree
and Allah was trying to prevent them eating
from this specific tree so that they would not live forever
and become elevated to the level of Angels.
In reality, his main goal was to retaliate against them for being
preferred over him and honored by Allah.

وأقسم لهما إبليس أنهما إذا أكلا من الشجرة المحرمة فسيصبحا ملكين
ويكونا من الخالدين،
وبالطبع كان هدفه الأساسى هو دفع آدم لمعصية الله
والأنتقام منه لتكريم الله له وتفضيله عليه.

**"Then Satan whispered suggestions to them in order
to reveal to them their shame that was hidden
from them (before); and he said: 'Your Lord did not forbid you
both from this tree except that you should become angels
or live forever.'" (Al-Araf:20)**

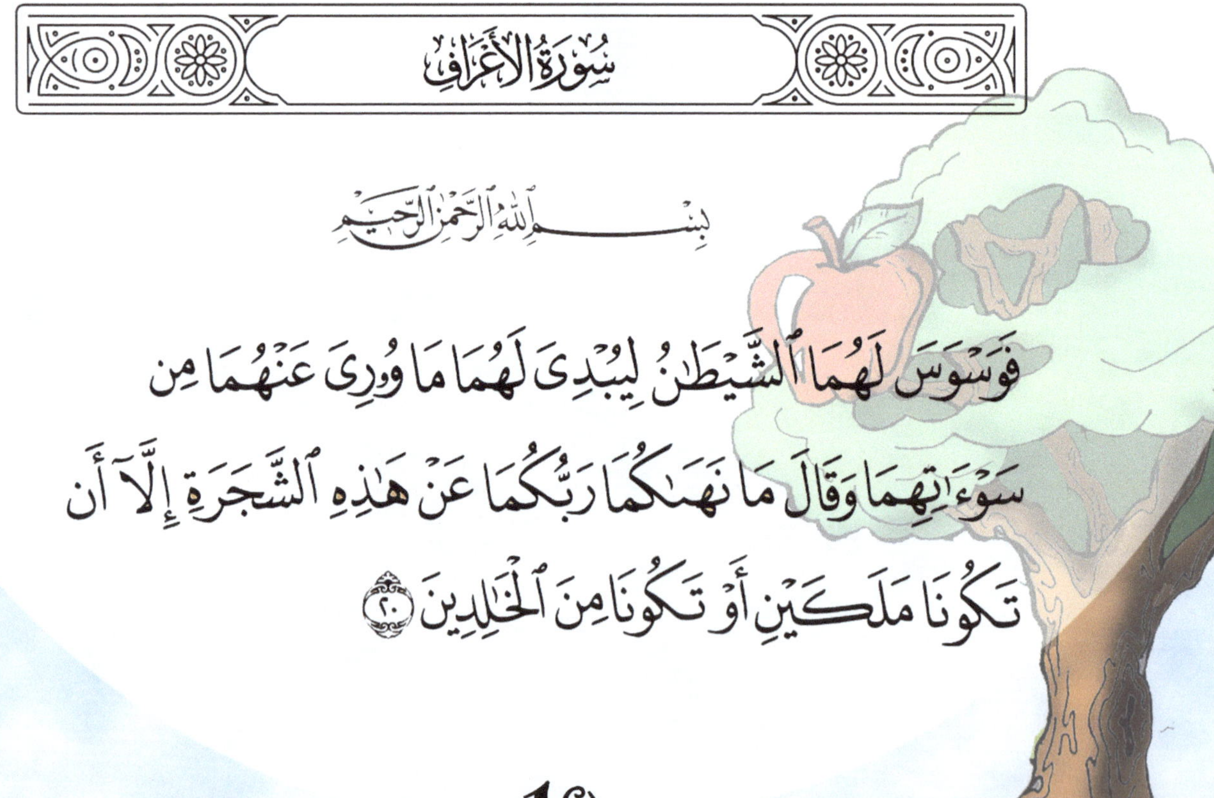

سُورَةُ الأَعْرَافِ

بِسْمِ اللهِ الرَّحْمَنِ الرَّحِيمِ

فَوَسْوَسَ لَهُمَا الشَّيْطَانُ لِيُبْدِيَ لَهُمَا مَا وُورِيَ عَنْهُمَا مِن
سَوْءَاتِهِمَا وَقَالَ مَا نَهَاكُمَا رَبُّكُمَا عَنْ هَذِهِ الشَّجَرَةِ إِلَّا أَن
تَكُونَا مَلَكَيْنِ أَوْ تَكُونَا مِنَ الْخَالِدِينَ ﴿٢٠﴾

After repeated attempts from Iblis,
Adam and Hawa finally ate from the forbidden tree
and instantly realized how wrong they were to do so.
They felt they had committed a huge sin by disobeying Allah
and falling for Iblis's temptations and deeply regretted
their wrong-doing.

وبعد محاولات عديدة من إبليس أكل آدم وحواء من الشجرة المحرمة
وشعرا حينها أنهما عصيا أمرِ الله وأستمعا لغواية الشيطان،
وآسفا أسفاً شديداً على معصيتهما
وندما كل الندم على أتباع نصائح إبليس والإنزلاق وراء إغراءاته.

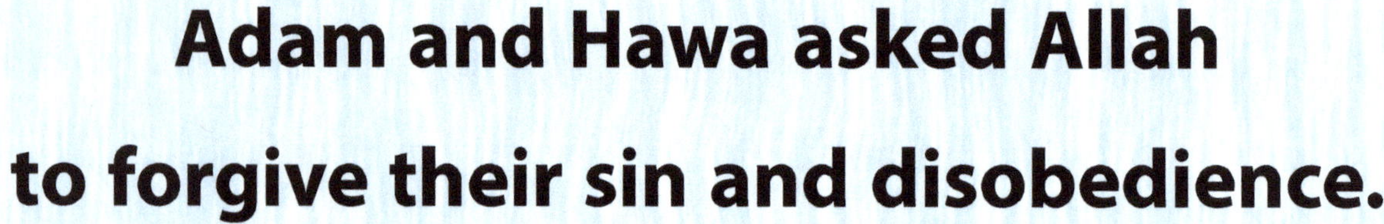

**Adam and Hawa asked Allah
to forgive their sin and disobedience.**

وعندها طلب آدم وحواء من الله أن يغفر لهما خطيأتهما.

"They said: `Our Lord! We have wronged ourselves.
If You forgive us not, and bestow not upon us Your Mercy,
we shall certainly be of the losers.' "
(Al-Araf: 23)

بِسْمِ اللهِ الرَّحْمَنِ الرَّحِيمِ

قَالَا رَبَّنَا ظَلَمْنَا أَنفُسَنَا وَإِن لَّمْ تَغْفِرْ لَنَا وَتَرْحَمْنَا لَنَكُونَنَّ مِنَ الْخَاسِرِينَ ۝

Allah accepted their repentance and regret,
but He made them leave Paradise and sent them
to Earth to live.

Allah reminded them, as well as their progeny, of Iblis's ill-will and
warned them of his treacherous ways and tricks.

فغفر لهما ربهما، وقال الآن أهبطا الى الأرض فلا مكان لكما بالجنة،
وعيشا على الأرض أنتم وعدوكم اللدود إبليس.
وتكاثروا فيها وسيكون إبليس وذريته عدواً دائماً لذرية بنى آدم،
فخذوا حذركم منه ومن إغراءاته هو وذريته.

As our Creator, Allah knows how difficult it can be for us
to resist Iblis's temptations and tricks.
Allah sent us the last Surah in the Qur'an, Surah al-Naas,
as a powerful tool to help us stay strong.
What a Merciful God! He knows our challenges and weaknesses,
and doesn't leave us on our own without His Guidance and Help.

والله بعد أن حذر الإنسان من عداوة الشيطان له أوضح لبنى آدم الوسيلة لإتقاء شره
ووسوسته، وهى ذكر الله والإستعانة بالله من شرور الشيطان ووساوسه،
وخير ما نختم به هو سورة الناس كعلاج واقى بإذن الله.
حقاً يا له من إله رحيم بعباده، عليم بضعف الإنسان وصراعاته
فلم يتركه وحيداً بلا توجيه منه.

"Say: `I seek refuge with

Allah the Lord of mankind(1)

The King of mankind-(2)

The God of mankind-(3)

From the mischief of the whisperer (of Evil),

who withdraws (after his whisper)(4)

Who whispers into the hearts of mankind (5)

Of jinn and men.' (6)"

(Al-Naas)

بِسۡمِ ٱللَّهِ ٱلرَّحۡمَٰنِ ٱلرَّحِيمِ

قُلۡ أَعُوذُ بِرَبِّ ٱلنَّاسِ ۝ مَلِكِ ٱلنَّاسِ ۝ إِلَٰهِ ٱلنَّاسِ ۝ مِن شَرِّ ٱلۡوَسۡوَاسِ ٱلۡخَنَّاسِ ۝ ٱلَّذِى يُوَسۡوِسُ فِى صُدُورِ ٱلنَّاسِ ۝ مِنَ ٱلۡجِنَّةِ وَٱلنَّاسِ ۝

We learn from this story to follow
Allah's commands, to stay away from
bad deeds, and not to follow our desires.
Even if we make a mistake, we must always
remember Allah and ask for forgiveness.
We should choose our friends carefully and try to find
others who will help us do good deeds.

ونستفيد من هذه القصة أن نتبع أوامر الله وأن نبتعد عن عمل السيئات وألا ننساق وراء الشهوات، كما علينا ذكر الله دائماً وطلب المغفرة عند الخطأ، والحرص في إختيار الأصدقاء الذين يشجعونا على العمل الصالح.

ISSA PBUH
عيسى عليه السلام
ILYAS PBUH
إلياس عليه السلام
MUHAMMAD PBUH
محمد عليه الصلاة والسلام
ZAKARIYA PBUH
زكريا عليه السلام
MUSA PBUH
موسى عليه السلام
ALYASA PBUH
اليسع عليه السلام
YAHYA PBUH
يحيى عليه السلام
SULAIMAN PBUH
سليمان عليه السلام
HAROON PBUH
هارون عليه السلام
YUSUF PBUH
يوسف عليه السلام
YUNUS PBUH
يونس عليه السلام
DAWOOD PBUH
داود عليه السلام
YAQUB PBUH
يعقوب عليه السلام
ISMAIL PBUH
إسماعيل عليه السلام
SHUAIB PBUH
شعيب عليه السلام
ISHAQ PBUH
إسحاق عليه السلام
DHUL KIFL PBUH
ذو الكفل عليه السلام
AYYUB PBUH
أيوب عليه السلام
IBRAHIM PBUH
إبراهيم عليه السلام
HUD PBUH
هود عليه السلام
LUT PBUH
لوط عليه السلام
NUH PBUH
نوح عليه السلام
SALIH PBUH
صالح عليه السلام
IDRIS PBUH
إدريس عليه السلام
ADAM PBUH
آدم عليه السلام
Adam PBUH is the Father of all humanity
آدم عليه السلام هو أبو البشرية

Watch a special reading of
Adam PBUH by the author!

Scan this QR code to access the video.

www.ingramcontent.com/pod-product-compliance
Lightning Source LLC
Chambersburg PA
CBHW042141030726

47599CB00002B/568